Newcastle United Quiz Book

101 Questions To Test Your Knowledge Of This Prestigious Club

Published by Glowworm Press
7 Nuffield Way
Abingdon OX14 1RL

By Chris Carpenter

Newcastle United

This book contains one hundred and one informative and entertaining trivia questions with multiple-choice answers about Newcastle United Football Club.

With 101 questions, some easy, some far harder, this entertaining book will test your knowledge and memory of the club's long and successful history. You will be asked a hatful of wonderful questions on a wide range of topics associated with Newcastle United FC for you to test yourself. You will be quizzed on players, legends, managers, opponents, transfer deals, trophies, records, honours, fixtures, songs and much more, guaranteeing you a fun and educational experience.

2021/22 Season Edition

FOREWORD

When I was asked to write a foreword to this book I was deeply honoured.

I have known the author Chris Carpenter for many years and his knowledge of facts and figures is phenomenal.

His love for football and the North East, and his talent for writing quiz books makes him the ideal man to pay homage to my great love Newcastle United Football Club.

This book came about as a result of a challenge in a Lebanese restaurant of all places!

I do hope you enjoy the book.

Colin Harper

Let's start with some relatively easy questions.

1. When were Newcastle United founded?
   A. 1882
   B. 1892
   C. 1902

2. What is Newcastle United's nickname?
   A. The Crows
   B. The Magpies
   C. The Ravens

3. Where do Newcastle United play their home games?
   A. St. James' Park
   B. St. Johns' Park
   C. St. Marys

4. What is the stadium's capacity?
   A. 50,053
   B. 51,530
   C. 52,305

5. Who or what is the club mascot?
   A. Mandy Magpie
   B. Mardy Magpie
   C. Monty Magpie

6. Who has made the most appearances for the club in total?
   A. Shay Given
   B. Frank Hudspeth
   C. Jimmy Lawrence

7. Who has made the most *League* appearances
   for the club?
      A. Jimmy Lawrence
      B. Bill McCracken
      C. Bobby Mitchell

8. Who is the club's record goal scorer?
      A. Jackie Milburn
      B. Alan Shearer
      C. Len White

9. Who is the fastest ever goal scorer for the
   club?
      A. Demba Ba
      B. Andy Cole
      C. Alan Shearer

10. Which of these is a well-known pub near
    the ground?
      A. The Magpie's Nest
      B. The Strawberry
      C. St. James' Tavern

OK, so here are the answers to the first ten questions. If you get eight or more right, you are doing very well so far, but the questions will get harder.

A1. Newcastle United was formed on 9th December 1892 following the merger of Newcastle East End and Newcastle West End, so the club is truly "United".

A2. Newcastle United are of course known as The Magpies, owing to their famous black and white home strip. Local fans also refer to the club as the toon.

A3. Newcastle plays their home games at the famous St. James' Park, and has done so since their foundation.

A4. The stadium has a capacity of 52,305, which is one of the largest in the country.

A5. It's only right that the mascot of The Magpies is, of course, Monty Magpie. Give yourself a bonus point if you knew he had a girlfriend called Maggie Magpie.

A6. Jimmy Lawrence holds the appearance record for the club, wearing the famous black and white shirt 496 times in his time at the club from 1904-1922. He would have played even more games if it wasn't for the First World War.

A7. Club legend Jimmy Lawrence made an impressive 432 appearances in the League for Newcastle between 1904 and 1922.

A8. Goal machine Alan Shearer is the top scorer in the club's history, notching 206 goals in all competitions, in his ten years at the club from 1996 to 2006.

A9. Alan Shearer also holds the fastest goal record, netting after just 10.4 seconds in a Premier League match against Manchester City on 18th January 2003.

A10. There are many watering holes in the city and near the ground which are good for pre and post match drinks. Despite its odd name, The Strawberry is the pub of choice for many of the Newcastle faithful on match days, with a lively atmosphere inside. Be prepared to queue for a pint though.

OK, back to the questions.

11. What is the highest number of goals that the club has scored in a league season?
    A. 98
    B. 99
    C. 100

12. What is the fewest number of goals that the club has conceded in a league season?
    A. 33
    B. 34
    C. 35

13. Who has scored the most penalties for the club?
    A. Frank Hudspeth
    B. Rob Lee
    C. Alan Shearer

14. What is the home end of the ground known as?
    A. East Stand
    B. Gallowgate End
    C. Milburn Stand

15. What is the club's record attendance?
    A. 68,386
    B. 69,386
    C. 70,386

16. What is the name of the road the ground is on?

A. Ballock Road
B. Barrack Road
C. Bedrock Road

17. What song do the players run out to?
    A. Back In Black – AC/DC
    B. Going Home – Mark Knopfler
    C. We Will Rock You - Queen

18. Which stand has the biggest capacity?
    A. East Stand
    B. Gallowgate
    C. Milburn Stand

19. What is the size of the pitch?
    A. 110x68 yards
    B. 112x70 yards
    C. 115x74 yards

20. Where is Newcastle United's training ground?
    A. Darsley Park
    B. Parsley Park
    C. Upton Park

Here are your answers to the last set of questions.

A11. Newcastle managed to score a whopping 98 goals in just 42 games in the old First Division in the 1951-52 season

A12. The club's best defensive campaign was in the 1904-05 season, when the defence conceded just 33 goals.

A13. Impossible to keep out of this quiz book, Alan Shearer holds the record for the most penalties scored for The Magpies, with 37 successful spot kicks in total.

A14. The home fans' end is of course the atmospheric Gallowgate End, where thousands of proud Geordies sit together on match days.

A15. A record 68,386 fans crammed into St James' Park to see Newcastle play Chelsea on 3rd September 1930.

A16. The ground is located on Barrack Road, right in the city centre.

A17. Newcastle players run out to the strains of local hero Mark Knopfler's anthem "Going Home".

A18. The Milburn stand (named after club legend Jackie) has the largest capacity, accommodating 14,844 fans, all seated.

A19. The playing surface at St James' Park is a whopping 115 yards long by 74 yards wide.

A20. Newcastle's training centre is located at Darsley Park, North Tyneside.

Here is the next set of questions.

21. What is the club's record win in any competition?
    A. 13-0
    B. 14-0
    C. 15-0

22. Who did they beat?
    A. Derby County
    B. Newport County
    C. Stockport County

23. In which season?
    A. 1946/47
    B. 1947/48
    C. 1948/49

24. What is the club's record defeat?
    A. 0-7
    B. 0-8
    C. 0-9

25. Who started the 2021/22 season as manager?
    A. Rafa Benitez
    B. Steve Bruce
    C. Steve McClaren

26. Who started the 2021/22 season as club captain?
    A. Ciaran Clark
    B. Jamaal Lascelles

C. Jonjo Shelvey

27. What shirt number does Isaac Hayden wear?
    A. 14
    B. 15
    C. 16

28. Who is the youngest player ever to represent the club?
    A. Sammy Ameobi
    B. Shane Ferguson
    C. Steve Watson

29. Who is the oldest player ever to represent the club?
    A. Peter Beardsley
    B. Billy Hampson
    C. Jimmy Stewart

30. Who has scored the most hat tricks for Newcastle United?
    A. Andy Cole
    B. Jackie Milburn
    C. Alan Shearer

Here are the answers to the last set of questions.

A21. Newcastle's record victory was a colossal 13-0 win.

A22. This massive 13-0 win came against Newport County.

A23. This match took place during the 1946/47 season, on 5th October 1946 in a league match in the old Division Two (now The Championship).

A24. Newcastle's worst ever defeat was a 9-0 loss, ouch! This defeat was suffered at the hands of Burton Wanderers on 15th April 1895, so a very long time ago.

A25. Steve Bruce started the 2021/22 season having been appointed to the job in July 2019.

A26. Multiple tattooed defender Jamaal Lascelles started the 2020/21 season as club captain.

A27. Midfielder Isaac Hayden wears shirt number 14.

A28. Steve Watson is the youngest player ever to play for The Magpies. He made his debut on 10th November 1990 against Wolverhampton Wanderers aged just 16 years and 223 days.

A29. Billy Hampson is the oldest player ever to represent The Magpies. He appeared against

Birmingham City on 9th April 1927 at the age of 42 years and 225 days.

A30. Legend and namesake of the Main Stand, Jackie Milburn has scored the most hat tricks for Newcastle with nine. This is three more than his closest rival.

Now we move onto some questions about the club's trophies.

31. How many times have Newcastle United won the League?
    A. 3
    B. 4
    C. 5

32. How many times have Newcastle United won the FA Cup?
    A. 4
    B. 5
    C. 6

33. How many times have the club won the League Cup?
    A. 0
    B. 2
    C. 4

34. How many times have the club won the Charity / Community Shield?
    A. 0
    B. 1
    C. 2

35. How many times have the club won a major European trophy?
    A. 0
    B. 1
    C. 2

36. When did the club win their first league title?
     A. 1904/05
     B. 1905/06
     C. 1906/07

37. When did the club win their first FA Cup?
     A. 1908
     B. 1910
     C. 1912

38. Who was the last captain to lift the League trophy?
     A. Fabricio Coloccini
     B. Hughie Gallacher
     C. Arthur Wharton

39. Who was the last captain to lift the FA Cup?
     A. Jock Rutherford
     B. Jimmy Scoular
     C. Colin Veitch

40. Who was the last captain to lift a major European Trophy?
     A. Frank Clark
     B. Wyn Davies
     C. Bobby Moncur

Here are your answers to the last set of questions.

A31. Newcastle United has won the League four times in total.

A32. Newcastle United has been engraved onto the FA Cup six times

A33. Newcastle has never won the League Cup, although they came close as runners-up in 1976.

A34. Newcastle United won the Charity Shield in 1909. Since then, the club has been runners up on five occasions.

A35. The club has won one major European Trophy – The Inter-Cities Fairs Cup, which was a predecessor to the EUFA Cup, which later became the Europa League.

A36. Newcastle won the first of their league titles in the 1904/05 season.

A37. The Magpies won their first FA Cup back in 1910, beating Barnsley 2-0 in a replay on 28th April 1910 at Goodison Park in Liverpool, after the first game finished 1-1 on 23rd April 1910 at the old Crystal Palace in London.

A38. Hughie Gallacher wore the captain's armband during the club's championship winning season in 1926/27.

A39. The last Newcastle captain to get his hands on the FA Cup was the tough tackling Jimmy Scoular, after a 3-1 victory over Manchester City at Wembley Stadium on 7th May 1955. Manchester City had worn flashy tracksuits, so the game was daubed as "the Gaudies vs the Geordies".

A40. Bobby Moncur was the captain of the 1969 Inter-Cities Fairs Cup winning side.

I hope you're having fun, and getting most of the answers right.

41. What is the record transfer fee paid?
    A. £30 million
    B. £35 million
    C. £40 million

42. Who was the record transfer fee paid for?
    A. Miguel Almiron
    B. Joelinton
    C. Joe Willock

43. What is the record transfer fee received?
    A. £15 million
    B. £25 million
    C. £35 million

44. Who was the record transfer fee received for?
    A. Yohan Cabaye
    B. Andy Carroll
    C. Moussa Sissoko

45. Who was the first Newcastle United player to play for England?
    A. Matthew Kingsley
    B. John Rutherford
    C. Albert Shepherd

46. Who has won the most international caps whilst a Newcastle United player?
    A. Shay Given

B. Kevin Keegan
C. Cheick Tiote

47. Who has scored the most international goals whilst a Newcastle United player?
    A. Faustino Asprilla
    B. Papiss Cisse
    C. Alan Shearer

48. What is the club's official website address?
    A. newcastlefc.co.uk
    B. newcastleunited.co.uk
    C. nufc.co.uk

49. What is the club's official twitter account?
    A. @NewcastleUnited
    B. @NUFC
    C. @NUFCOfficial

50. Who is considered as Newcastle United's main rivals?
    A. Hartlepool
    B. Middlesbrough
    C. Sunderland

Here are the answers to the last set of questions.

A41. The club's record transfer paid for one player is £40 million.

A42. This fee was paid for Brazilian forward Joelinton, who arrived from Hoffenheim in July 2019. This eclipsed the previous record of £21 million paid for Miguel Almiron, who arrived in January 2019.

A43. The largest transfer fee the club has received for one player is £35 million.

A44. Liverpool paid this enormous amount to secure the services of local boy Andy Carroll, in January 2011.

A45. Matthew Kingsley was the first Newcastle player to be capped for England way back in 1901.

A46. Shay Given made a record 80 international appearances for the Republic of Ireland while playing for The Magpies.

A47. Alan Shearer scored 25 of his 30 international goals while playing for Newcastle.

A48. nufc.co.uk is the club's official website address. This is not to be confused with the unofficial website at nufc.com.

A49. @NUFC is the club's official twitter account. It tweets multiple times daily and it has almost two million followers.

A50. Despite there being a few teams in the North East of England, Newcastle's bitterest rivalry is with Sunderland, making for some pulsating matches over the years.

I hope you're learning some new facts about the Magpies.

51. Who is Newcastle United's oldest ever goal scorer?
    A. John Barnes
    B. Peter Beardsley
    C. Ivan Broadis

52. Who is the club's longest serving manager of all time?
    A. Richard Dinnis
    B. Joe Harvey
    C. George Martin

53. Who is the only Newcastle manager who has won the Premier League Manager of the Season award?
    A. Alan Pardew
    B. Bobby Robson
    C. Graeme Souness

54. Who was the manager when the club finished Premier League runners up in 1996?
    A. Kenny Dalglish
    B. Ruud Gullit
    C. Kevin Keegan

55. What is the name of the Newcastle United match day programme?
    A. Black and White
    B. The Magpies

C. United

56. Which of these is a Newcastle United fanzine?
    A. Fog on the Tyne
    B. Magpie News
    C. True Faith

57. What animals are on the club crest?
    A. Lions
    B. Seahorses
    C. Zebras

58. What is the club's motto?
    A. Audere est facere
    B. Fortiter defendit triumphans
    C. Nils satis nisi optimum

59. Which former England boss became manager of the club in 1999?
    A. Kevin Keegan
    B. Steve McClaren
    C. Sir Bobby Robson

60. What could be regarded as the club's most well-known song?
    A. Blaydon Races
    B. House of the Rising Sun
    C. Unchained Melody

Here are the answers to the last block of questions.

A51. Peter Beardsley is the oldest player to net for The Magpies, scoring at the ripe old age of 36 years and 56 days in a 4-0 victory over Coventry City in a Premier League match on 15th March 1997.

A52. Joe Harvey is the longest serving manager in the club's history, and was in charge for 591 matches in total from June 1962 to June 1975.

A53. Alan Pardew won the Premier League Manager of the Season award in 2012. It was an odd choice in many ways, as the club finished in fifth position in the league, some 24 points behind the champions Manchester City.

A54. Kevin Keegan was the manager when the club finished runners up in the Premier League in 1996. The brand of football the club played under Keegan was at times breath-taking and very exciting, with the team being dubbed 'The Entertainers'. The following season, after Keegan quit in January 1997, the club went on to finish runners-up again, with Kenny Dalglish at the helm for the last few months of the season.

A55. The club's official match day programme is simply called "United".

A56. There are a number of fanzines, but arguably the best known is called True Faith.

A57. The easily recognisable club crest features a black and white striped shield flanked by two seahorses.

A58. The team's Latin motto is "fortiter defendit triumphans", which in English means "Triumphing by brave defence".

A59. Sir Bobby Robson returned to his native Tyneside in 1999, and enjoyed a successful spell as manager for a number of years.

A60. Blaydon Races is a famous Geordie folk song from the 19th century, and it is a song that is sung with pride by Newcastle fans, both home and away.

Let's give you some easier questions.

61. What is the traditional colour of the home
    shirt?
       A. Black and White
       B. Black and Red
       C. Black and Blue

62. What is the traditional colour of the away
    shirt?
       A. Green
       B. Pink
       C. Yellow

63. Who is the current club sponsor?
       A. Fun88
       B. Sports Direct
       C. Wonga

64. Who was the first club sponsor?
       A. Greenalls Beers
       B. Newcastle Breweries
       C. McEwan's Lager

65. Which of these once sponsored the club?
       A. Virgin Atlantic
       B. Virgin Cola
       C. Virgin Money

66. Who is currently the club chairman?
       A. Mike Ashley
       B. Steve Gibson
       C. Niall Quinn

67. Who was the club's first foreign signing?
     A. Edwin Dutton
     B. David Ginola
     C. Pavel Srnicek

68. Who was the club's first black player?
     A. Howard Gayle
     B. Cyrille Regis
     C. Arthur Wharton

69. Who was the club's first match in the league against?
     A. Wolverhampton Wanderers
     B. Woolwich Arsenal
     C. Workington

70. How many players won the PFA Player of the Year award whilst playing for the club?
     A. 1
     B. 2
     C. 3

Here is the latest set of answers.

A61. Anyone who gets this wrong should stop this quiz right now. BLACK AND WHITE are of course the colours of the mighty Magpies!

A62. The truth is that Newcastle have never had a consistent away shirt colour, and it changes almost every season (a cunning money making trick perhaps). Since 1995, the kit has not been the same for more than a single season.

A63. The current shirt sponsor is Chinese gaming firm Fun88. The contract does not include naming rights to the ground.

A64. The club's first ever shirt sponsor was with Scottish and Newcastle Breweries in 1980. This was in the day when Newcastle Brown Ale was brewed in the toon.

A65. After taking over Northern Rock, Virgin Money sponsored the club from 2012 to 2013.

A66. The current chairman at St James' Park is sports retail kingpin Mike Ashley, who became chairman in 2007 and it is fair to say that his time in charge has not been without controversy.

A67. Edwin Dutton was a German footballer before and after the First World War, who played for Newcastle in the 1918/19 season.

A68. Goalkeeper Arthur Wharton played for The Magpies all the way back in the 1880's, and he has been recognised by FIFA as the first ever black professional footballer anywhere!

A69. Newcastle United's first ever game in the old Second Division took place against Woolwich Arsenal on 30th September 1893. The match finished 2-2.

A70. Two players have won the coveted PFA Player of the Year award whilst playing for Newcastle United; Les Ferdinand won it in 1996 and Alan Shearer in 1997.

This next set of questions should test even the biggest fan.

71. Which striker holds the record for most goals in all competitions in a single season?
    A. Andy Cole
    B. Jackie Milburn
    C. George Robledo

72. Which player holds the record for most league goals in a single season?
    A. Demba Ba
    B. Hughie Gallacher
    C. Barrie Thomas

73. Which goalkeeper has kept the most clean-sheets for the club in the league?
    A. Shay Given
    B. Matt Kingsley
    C. Tim Krul

74. Who is the club's current kit supplier?
    A. Adidas
    B. Castore
    C. Puma

75. Who has scored the most goals in a single match for Newcastle United?
    A. Andy Cole
    B. Paul Gascoigne
    C. Len Shackleton

76. When did Newcastle United first use a
    plane to transport the team?
    A. 1958
    B. 1968
    C. 1978

77. Who is the youngest scorer for Newcastle
    United in European football?
    A. Darren Ambrose
    B. Alan Foggon
    C. Charles N'Zogbia

78. Against whom did Newcastle United win
    their only FA Charity Shield in 1909?
    A. Northampton Town
    B. Northwich Victoria
    C. Notts County

79. How many times has the club been involved
    in the UEFA Champions League?
    A. 1
    B. 2
    C. 3

80. Who was in charge of the club when they
    were relegated to the Championship in
    2009?
    A. Alan Hansen
    B. Alan Irvine
    C. Alan Shearer

Here are the answers to the last set of questions.

A71. Andy Cole holds the record for most goals in a season, scoring 41 times in total (including cup games) during the 1993/94 season.

A72. Hughie Gallacher holds the record for most league goals, scoring 36 goals in the 1926/27 season.

A73. Irishman Shay Given kept a record 91 clean sheets in total for The Magpies in League fixtures.

A74. The club's current kit manufacturer is Castore following a deal signed in July 2021. This followed many years with Puma supplying the kit.

A75. Len Shackleton holds the record for most goals in a single game, scoring six against Newport County in the famous 13-0 mauling on 5th October 1946.

A76. Newcastle United first flew their players home from a game back in 1958, after a match in Birmingham.

A77. Alan Foggon is the youngest ever scorer for The Magpies in a European match, netting against Vitoria Setubal in a European Fairs Cup match on 12th March 1969 aged just 19 years and 17 days.

A78. Northampton Town were the losers in the 1909 FA Charity Shied as Newcastle claimed their only victory in this annual fixture.

A79. Newcastle have played in the UEFA Champions League on two occasions, in the 1997/98 and 2002/03 seasons but both times did not make it to the knockout stage of the competition.

A80. Club legend Alan Shearer was unable to prevent his hometown club from relegation, after he took over as interim boss in the final stages of the 2008/09 season, following Joe Kinnear's heart problems which forced him to step down.

Onto the next set of questions.

81. Who has scored the most European goals for Newcastle United?
    A. Shola Ameobi
    B. David Ginola
    C. Alan Shearer

82. Who has scored the most goals against bitter rivals Sunderland?
    A. Faustino Asprilla
    B. Rob Lee
    C. Jackie Milburn

83. Who did Newcastle United record their famous comeback from 4-0 down to draw 4-4 in 2011?
    A. Arsenal
    B. Chelsea
    C. Liverpool

84. Who managed Newcastle United between 1892 and 1930?
    A. Andy Cunningham
    B. Tom Mather
    C. Neither

85. Against whom did Alan Shearer score his last ever goal for the club?
    A. Stoke City
    B. Sunderland
    C. Swansea City

86. What is the greatest number of penalties given away by Newcastle United in a single season in the Premier League?
    A. 7
    B. 9
    C. 11

87. Which of these celebrities is a famous Newcastle United fan?
    A. Brian Blessed
    B. Brian May
    C. Brian Johnson

88. Who was the opposition in the last England game to be held at St James' Park?
    A. Andorra
    B. Argentina
    C. Azerbaijan

89. How many seasons have Newcastle United spent in the top-flight of English football?
    A. 81
    B. 84
    C. 87

90. What is the highest number of consecutive seasons that Newcastle United has spent in the top division?
    A. 30
    B. 35
    C. 40

Here are the answers to the last set of questions.

A81. Top European goal scorer is another of Alan Shearer's records, with the forward having hit the target on 30 occasions against foreign opposition.

A82. Club hero Jackie Milburn is the undisputed king of the North East derby with eleven goals in matches against Sunderland.

A83. One of the most exciting games in recent history was the 4-4 thriller against Arsenal on 5th February 2011 when the Toon came back from 0-4 down to draw 4-4, with Tiote's volley the pick of the goals.

A84. Strangely, Newcastle United didn't have a manager between their entrance to the Football League and January 1930. A selection committee made up of several people picked the team.

A85. Shearer's final Newcastle goal was scored from the penalty spot in a 4-1 win over rivals Sunderland at the Stadium of Light on 17th April 2006.

A86. Newcastle United gave nine penalties away on two occasions in the Premier League (2008/09 and 2011/12).

A87. One of Newcastle United's most famous celebrity fans is AC/DC frontman Brian Johnson, who grew up in the North East of England.

A88. The last England fixture to be played at St James' Park was against Azerbaijan on 30th March 2005, in which The Three Lions were 2-0 victors.

A89. The 2019/20 season is Newcastle United's 87th season in the top tier of football in England.

A90. Newcastle's longest consecutive spell in the top division of English football is 35 seasons. This occurred between 1899 and 1934.

You have reached the final furlong. Here we go.

91. How many players have won the PFA Player of the Year Award whilst playing for Newcastle United?
    A. 2
    B. 3
    C. 4

92. How many players have won the PFA Young Player of the Year Award whilst playing for Newcastle United?
    A. 4
    B. 5
    C. 6

93. What relation are the Charlton brothers, Bobby and Jack, to Newcastle United legend Jackie Milburn?
    A. Cousins
    B. Nephews
    C. Stepbrothers

94. What nationality is Allan Saint-Maximin?
    A. Austrian
    B. French
    C. German

95. Which flamboyant French midfielder joined the club in the mid-1990s?
    A. David Ginola
    B. Emmanuel Petit
    C. Robert Pires

96. Against whom did Newcastle United play
their last match in a European competition?
    A. Bayern Munich
    B. Benfica
    C. Braga

97. How many seasons have Newcastle United
featured in European cup competitions?
    A. 15
    B. 16
    C. 17

98. What was the aggregate score in the 1969
Fairs Cup final against Ujpesti Dozsa?
    A. 3-0
    B. 3-2
    C. 6-2

99. What is Newcastle United's biggest victory
in the Premier League era?
    A. 6-0
    B. 7-0
    C. 8-0

100. Which former player is honoured with a
statue outside St James' Park?
    A. Joe Harvey
    B. Kevin Keegan
    C. Alan Shearer

101. Which former manager is honoured with a
statue outside St James' Park?

A. Bobby Robson
B. Glenn Roeder
C. Graeme Souness

Here are the answers to the final set of questions.

A91. Two players have won the coveted PFA player of the year award whilst playing for Newcastle United; Les Ferdinand (1996) and Alan Shearer (1997).

A92. Four of Newcastle's young stars have been awarded the PFA young player of the year award: Paul Gascoigne, Andy Cole, Craig Bellamy and Jermaine Jenas.

A93. Two of England's best players, the Charlton brothers, are in fact nephews of arguably The Magpies most popular player ever, Jackie Milburn.

A94.Winger Saint-Maximin was born in France.

A95. David Ginola moved to Newcastle from Paris Saint-Germain in the summer of 1995 and quickly became a fans' favourite at St James' Park amongst both male and female supporters.

A96. Newcastle reached the quarter finals of the Europa League in 2012/13, losing out to Benfica 2-4 on aggregate.

A97. The Toon have featured in European cup football 17 times.

A98. The Magpies won the 1969 Fairs Cup after beating Ujpesti Dozsa 6-2 over two legs. Newcastle won the home leg 3-0 on 29th May and won the second leg in Hungary 3-2 on 11th June.

A99. The Toon's biggest win in the Premier League came against Sheffield Wednesday on 19th September 1999, with Newcastle romping to an 8-0 victory.

A100. A nine feet six inches tall statue of legend Shearer was unveiled by the man himself on 12th September 2016. The statue was funded by former chairman Freddy Shepherd.

A101. A statue of former Newcastle and England manager Sir Bobby Robson was unveiled outside St James' Park in May 2012.

That's it. That's a great question to finish with. I hope you enjoyed this book, and I hope you got most of the answers right.

I also hope you learnt some new facts about the club, and if you saw anything wrong, or have a general comment, please visit the glowwormpress.com website.

Thanks for reading, and if you did enjoy the book, would you be so kind as leave a positive review on Amazon.

Printed in Great Britain
by Amazon

72302012R00028